by

Gerald Mack

GPBM Publications

8730 Cincinnati-Dayton Rd. #755 West Chester, OH 45069

Manufactured in the United States Of America

Cover design: **Ges**

Editor: **Ges**

ISBN 979-8-218-30418-8

Library of Congress has cataloged: Gerald Mack: Middie Mindset / 1't. ed.

p. cm.

2 0 2 3 9 2 0 9 4 4

This publication is designed to provide accurate and authoritative information in regards to the subject matter covered. It is sold with the understanding that the publisher is not engaged in rendering legal, accounting, or other professional services. If you require legal advice or other expert assistance, you should seek the services of a competent professional.

Contents

Individually you have to take the first step into building your own mindset.

–G, Mack

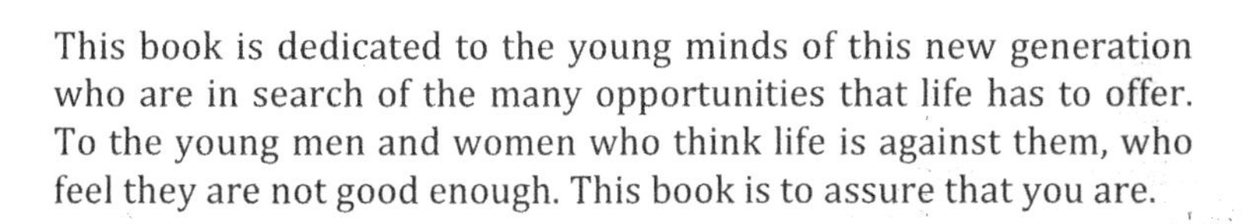

This book is dedicated to the young minds of this new generation who are in search of the many opportunities that life has to offer. To the young men and women who think life is against them, who feel they are not good enough. This book is to assure that you are.

To those who lack the proper tutelage from teachers, parents, peers and lack mentorship.

This book is dedicated to the young minds ready for a reset. However, do understand the resetting of your mindset is not an event, it is a process.

One of the greatest temptations is to ease up a little bit. –W, Isdom

Prologue
Embody The Middie Mindset

Welcome to the exhilarating journey of self-discovery and personal growth! The years you spend in high school are some of the most transformative and defining moments of your life. As you embark on this adventure, I will present to you the keys to unlock your potential, rid self-doubt, lazy thinking and introduce you to the dopest mindset that you will thank me for later.

In the bustling corridors of high schools, where dreams and ambitions intermingle with uncertainties and low self-esteem, there lies a unique approach to life—a mindset that we shall call the "Middie Mindset." This mindset is not about being in the middle of the pack or settling for mediocrity; rather, it's a powerful perspective that empowers high school students to navigate the many challenges of adolescence with resilience, purpose, and self-assurance.

High school, as many will attest, is a period of immense change and growth—a transformative phase where individuals seek to define themselves and uncover their passions and talents. Amidst the pressures of academic performance, social expectations, and future aspirations, it's easy for students to feel overwhelmed, lost, or inadequate. This is where the Middie Mindset will soon come into play.

The Middie Mindset is rooted in the understanding that every student is unique, with their own strengths, weaknesses, and journey. It encourages individuals to break free from the shackles or comparison and self-doubt, realizing that they do not have to be the best at everything to lead fulfilling lives. The goal is to buy into the belief system that always angles the focus on honing in on their own abilities and becoming the best version of themselves.

In this journey of self-discovery, the Middie Mindset embraces the notion of learning from failures and setbacks. It reminds students that setbacks are not signs of defeat but stepping-stones towards growth. Embracing failures not only fosters resilience but also encourages a spirit of curiosity, motivating students to keep pushing their boundaries and exploring uncharted territories.

Moreover, the Middie Mindset emphasizes the significance of a supportive community. High school can be a maze of complex relationships, where friendships can be both a source of joy and pain. Students are encouraged to build a network of like-minded individuals who lift them up, cheer them on, and believe in their potential. By nurturing positive relationships, students can thrive in an environment that encourages collaboration, empathy, and understanding.

At the heart of the Middie Mindset is the realization that growth is a continuous process, and it's okay to be a work in progress. Let's repeat that, ***and it's okay to be to work in progress.*** Self-compassion and self-acceptance become cornerstones of this mindset, allowing students to let go of the pressures to be perfect and embrace their imperfections as part of their unique identity.

As we delve into the lives of high school students who embody the Middie Mindset, we will encounter stories of perseverance, courage, and determination. Please note that it is not always about reaching the top, but finding joy and fulfillment in the journey itself. As we begin to adopt the Middie Mindset we must first embrace challenges and embrace the uncertainties of life with open arms, knowing that each step no matter how small contributes to personal growth and character development.

Dear reader, as we embark on this exploration of the Middie Mindset, let us open our hearts and minds to impute wisdom. Whether you are a high school student trying to navigate the complexities of adolescence or a caring adult seeking to support and understand the youth, this mindset has the potential to ignite a spark of resilience and purpose within all of us, so let the journey begin!

Chapter 1

Embrace The Beginning of Learning

Hey there, fellow high schoolers! Welcome to the exciting world of learning and self-discovery. As you embark on this incredible journey I pray that you will adhere and adopt the **'Middie Mindset,'** –an attitude that embraces the beginning of learning and all the wonderful opportunities it brings. Whether you are a freshman, sophomore, junior, or senior, this mindset will help you make the most of your high school experience and set you up for success in the years to come. Throughout this book we will break down each topic giving you an opportunity to understand the different meanings and vitals in order for you to gradually grow. With that being said let's get to work.

1. Embrace Curiosity:

As a teenager in high school, you're at a pivotal point in your life where you have the chance to explore various subjects, interests, and hobbies. Embrace curiosity and be open to trying new things. Don't be afraid to ask questions, even if you think they might sound silly. Remember, curiosity is the driving force behind learning. It sparks your desire to understand the world and opens doors to endless possibilities.

2. Embrace Challenges:

Learning can be tough, and sometimes you might face challenges that seem insurmountable. But fear not! Embrace those challenges as opportunities to grow and improve. Whether it's tackling a difficult math problem, preparing for a presentation, or mastering a musical instrument, every challenge you conquer will make you stronger and more resilient. ***The journey is just as important as the destination, so celebrate your progress along the way.***

3. Embrace Failure:

Failure is a natural part of the learning process. It is okay to stumble and make mistakes; in fact, it's necessary for growth. Instead of seeing failure as something negative, view it as a stepping-stone towards success. Learn from your mistakes, adjust your approach, and keep moving forward. Remember, even the most successful people in the world have experienced failure at some point of time in their lives. *(Important.)*

4. Embrace Feedback:

Feedback is a valuable gift to help you understand your strengths and areas for improvement. Whether it comes from teachers, peers, or mentors, listen to feedback with an open mind and a growth-oriented attitude. Use feedback as a tool to refine your skills and knowledge continuously. Constructive criticism can lead to significant breakthroughs in your learning journey. **Be careful to only accept feedback pertaining to the answer you are hoping for.*

5. Embrace Collaboration:

High school is an excellent time to build strong relationships and learn from one another. Collaborating with your classmates can enrich your understanding of different subjects and perspectives. Engage in group discussions, study sessions, and team projects. Not only will you learn from your peers, but you will also develop essential teamwork and communication skills that will serve you well in the future.

6. Embrace Resilience:

In the pursuit of knowledge, you might face setbacks or encounter moments of self-doubt. However, remember that resilience is the key to overcoming these challenges. Keep pushing forward, stay determined, and believe in your ability to achieve your goals. Believe in yourself, and you will be amazed at what you can accomplish. *(Key Component.)*

7. Embrace Growth:

The Middie Mindset is all about continuous growth and improvement. As you learn, you will discover new passions and interests, and your perspectives will evolve. Embrace this transformation and be open to the idea that your goals and aspirations may change over time. Embrace the excitement of self-discovery, and welcome the person you are becoming.

8. Embrace YOU:

Being a teenager is a transformative journey that involves accepting and celebrating both strengths and vulnerabilities. It is a time of self-discovery, where learning to appreciate unique qualities and quirks fosters a sense of self-confidence. By embracing authenticity about you will build genuine connections with others and cultivate a positive self-image. This process involves acknowledging imperfections as stepping-stones to growth and understanding that self-worth goes beyond societal expectations. Embracing YOU empowers YOU to navigate challenges with resilience, develop healthy relationships, and pave the way for a fulfilling adulthood based on self-love and self-acceptance. *Note: *This is vital to the Middie Mindset.* ***Embrace YOU. Love YOU,*** no *matter what!*

The Middie Mindset is not just about the beginning of learning; **it's about sustaining a lifelong love for learning.** By embracing curiosity, challenges, failure, feedback, collaboration, resilience, and growth, you will not only excel in high school but also develop a strong foundation for your future endeavors. Embrace the journey, and remember that learning is a lifelong adventure filled with wonders waiting to be explored. So, my fellow high schoolers, let's Embrace the Middie Mindset and make the most of this incredible phase in your journey!

The journey of a thousand miles begins with one step. –Lao Tzu

Chapter 2

Understanding The Journey

The journey of being a teenager is often characterized by a rollercoaster of emotions and experiences, with both ups and downs. This period of life is a critical and transformative phase that bridges the gap between childhood and adulthood.

The Middie Mindset journey for teenagers is innovative and empowering, designed to guide adolescents through a transformative exploration of self-discovery and personal growth. Tailored to the unique challenges and opportunities that come with the nurturing mental, emotional, and social well-being. Participants embark on a dynamic adventure that encourages them to embrace their individuality, develop critical life skills, and cultivate resilience.

Throughout the Middie Mindset journey you will engage in a series of interactive experiences, reflective struggles, unrecognized victories, and peer led group discussions. These growth encounters gives life to a deep understanding of self-esteem, emotional intelligence, and healthy relationships. Guided by experienced mentors and facilitators many of you will learn how to navigate the complexities of your changing identities while building a strong foundation for future success. By taking notice to open communication, empathy, and promoting self-acceptance, this journey empowers all age groups to confidently face challenges, make informed decisions, and develop a positive sense of self as you transition into young adulthood. Here are some common aspects of the up and down journey as a teenager.

1. **Physical Changes:** One of the first major changes experienced during adolescence is puberty. This can lead to a mixture of excitement and confusion as you navigate the physical changes internal and externally.

2. **Emotional Turmoil:** Most teenagers will experience intense emotions and mood swings. You may feel happy and optimistic one moment, and then become upset of frustrated the next. These emotional ups and downs can be attributed to hormonal changes as well as the challenges of self-discovery.

3. **Identity Formation:** As you approach the teenage years, something happens and you begin to try and figure out who you are. You experiment with different styles, interests, and friendships. This exploration can be both exciting and overwhelming as you search for a sense of belonging and self-identity.

4. **Peer Pressure:** The inevitable, that thing that causes certain behaviors, habits, or social norms. This pressure can lead to difficult decisions and sometimes push you into uncomfortable situations.

5. **Academic Pressures:** The academic demands in a teenager's life can cause stress and anxiety. Balancing schoolwork, extracurricular activities, and social life can be challenging and lead to periods of feeling overwhelmed.

6. **Family Dynamics:** The dynamic between teenagers and their parents or guardians can be complicated. As teens seek more independence and autonomy, conflicts and disagreements may arise.

7. **Romantic Relationships:** Most teenagers will experience their first romantic relationships during this time. While falling in love can be exciting, it can also bring heartbreak and emotional vulnerability

8. **Self-Esteem Issues:** Body image concerns and comparisons to others may lead to struggles with self-esteem. You might feel insecure about your appearance or abilities. **God only created one of you, learn to love your uniqueness.** (*You're Wonderfully Created.)*

9. **Exploration of Risky Behaviors:** Some teenagers may engage in risky behaviors like substance use, reckless driving, or unprotected sex. These actions can have serious consequences and are often influenced by peer pressure and a desire for thrill-seeking.

10. **Personal Growth and Achievements:** Amidst the challenges, you are going to experience personal growth and accomplishments. They may come by way of academics, sports, arts, or other interests, leading to a boost in confidence and self-worth. *(own it.)*

11. **Social Life:** It's healthy to create and enjoy a vibrant social life filled with opportunities, obtaining resources, making new friends and creating lasting memories with peers. *(Responsibly)*

12. **Planning For The Future:** As you approach the end of your teenage years, make time to start considering your future career paths and life goals. This can bring excitement about possibilities and in turn decrease anxieties about making the right choices.

It is important to recognize that the teenage journey is unique for each individual. Some may face more ups than downs, while others may encounter greater challenges. Supportive relationships, open communication with parents or mentors, and access to mental health resources can all be instrumental in helping you as a teenager navigate through this transformative time with greater resilience and confidence.

Before moving on to the next chapter feel free to note what stood out to you and how it can help you grow along your journey.

Note:

____

____

____

____

____

Document The Times

Name:____

Date:____

Age:____

Grade:____

School:____

GPA:____

Current Commitments:

____

____

____

Social Involvement:

____

____

____

Hobbies:

____

____

____

Current Goals:

____

____

____

Current Mindset:

____

____

____

Current Core Beliefs:

____

____

____

____

Chapter 3

SHORTCUTS

There is an old wise saying, *'the longest way to your destiny is by taking the shortcut.'*

How so? Aren't shortcuts supposed to make the trip, the journey easier? Make it quicker to reach the destination? One would think so using a corner-cut mindset. Shortcuts can be a bad idea because they often sacrifice quality and thoroughness. They might lead to errors, overlooked details, or missed opportunities for improvement. Taking the time to do things properly usually yields better outcomes in the long run.

At an early age some where along the way many of us develop a Corner-Cut Mindset (CCM). We are oblivious to the habits that we adopt on a daily basis. Rather good or bad, they are formed everyday. Without knowing the severity of habits they can take us on many detours in life ultimately leading us down a road that requires extreme amounts of discipline to break them.

Let's say your mother sends you to the store. There are two ways you know to reach the destination.

1. Take the main road.
2. Cut through a few houses.

So you decide to cut through a few houses on the way to the store. All the while the main road is only a five-minute difference to the destination. You cut through the yard of the first house and things are going ok. Then comes house number two and you come face-to-face with an untrained, vicious Pit-bull. You are stunned and make a dash for the fence. Nevertheless, the Pit-bull is able to bite your Achilles tendon before you are able to clear the fence. This result to surgery and in walks the doctor, “I'm sorry to inform you, but you will not be able to return to sports until late next year.” Next year! You are going into your senior year and your full-ride scholarship is riding on your upcoming performances. Chances are you may never properly recover from your injury and the schools who were interested in you will simply state, “sorry, but we are now looking at someone else.”

So here we have a snap shot of what the longest way to your destiny taking the shortcut looks like. Ask yourself thus far, how many shortcuts have you taken? Were they worth it? Will you continue to take them or will you stay the course and take the main road?

Notes:

____
____
____
____
____
____
____
____
____
____
____
____
____
____
____
____
____
____
____
____
____

**When noting please be one hundred percent honest with yourself. Throughout this book you will have opportunities to journal. Please understand that it only works through honesty.*

Why is it so important to stay on the main course and not take shortcuts?

- What if doctors took shortcuts? How would that look during a heart or brain surgery?
- Most of today's youth enjoy video games, smart phones, and tablets. What if the programmers of those games, devices, decided to take shortcuts?
- Lets say you type in your destination on Google Maps and it takes you the opposite way. Will you be happy?

Now aren't we happy that the designers of the I-Phone, PlayStation, Computers and other gadgets did not take shortcuts. I too was once a teenager, therefore I understand that adjusting your thinking to stay the course and go the distance does not happen overnight, **it's a process!**

As you begin your journey to greatness it is imperative that you adopt willingness. Willingness will not allow you to cheat. It will always tell you to go the extra mile. Push yourself to the limit. Shoot 10 more shots. Run one more lap. These are personal attributes that you must have in order to obtain a Middie Mindset. On the contrary not all shortcuts are inherently bad; some can be useful when used appropriately and thoughtfully. However, those are not the shortcuts that I am referring to. By now you have the ability to use common sense and understand that sound judgment will always alert you when you are about to take a shortcut that is going to hurt you in the long run.

As a junior in high school I was a pretty-good 400-meter runner. I could run a sub 50, 51 in basketball shoes. However I'll be the first to admit, I was not a fan of lifting weights or rigorous training. Suffering from the illusion of control, I felt as if I could just show up and perform at a high level. I can remember our track coach telling us to run to the Burger King and back. (3.2) miles round trip.

Halfway through the run I would find a hiding spot. It would not be until I saw my teammates who actually ran to the Burger King and were on the way back that I would slip back into the pack and act as if I made the full run. At the time I thought it was ok. *Why do I need to run to the Burger King, I don't run cross country,* were my thoughts. Nevertheless come Saturday mornings when it was my turn to get into the blocks I would become nervous.

- Why was I nervous?
- I could run 50, 51 seconds in basketball shoes.
- I didn't have to lift weighs nor train hard.
- I could take shortcuts and not run to the Burger King.
- I could just show up.

Again, why was I nervous? Was it because I saw opponents who had more of a muscular build than myself? Was it the confident look my opponents held? Was it because I knew in my heart I had not put in the work?

Yes [ ] **No [ ]** **All of Above [X]**

Most of my races I would lose to guys who ran 49's, 50's and 51's. Were they faster, stronger or just that much better than me? No. But what they were was more focused. They ran all the way to the Burger King. They practiced humility and listened to their coaches. They trained harder. Those attributes and mindset allowed them to be one second faster than me. It is the little things that we do not do in life, do not pay attention to that will allow the opponent to be "1" second, "1" catch, "1" shot, "1" goal better than you.

Starting today we are going to focus forward and adopt the Middie Mindset's first rule of thumb, and that is in order to make it to our destination we will eliminate shortcuts from our thoughts and always give 110% effort in order to get the best results. **Never cheat you!!**

'the longest way to your destiny is by taking the shortcut'.

Chapter 4

Mastering Time Management

With the myriad of responsibilities in high school - academics, extracurricular activities and social life, effective time management is key. This chapter will equip you with practical tools and techniques to optimize your time, strike a balance between work and play, and eliminate procrastination.

Time management is a crucial skill during your teenage years. It is highly important for you to understand how to balance academics, extracurricular activities, social life, and personal interests effectively. Developing good time management skills at a young age sets a strong foundation for success in the future. Here are some important rules for improving time management skills.

1. **Set Clear Goals**:

   The first thing you must do is to set specific, realistic, and achievable goals for yourself. Whether it's completing homework, studying for exams, or pursuing new hobbies. Having clear objectives will give you direction.

2. **Prioritize Tasks:**

   Learn to prioritize tasks based on deadlines, importance, and urgency. Understanding what needs to be done first can prevent you from feeling overwhelmed which will promote a hyper-focus on essential activities.

3. **Create a Schedule:**

   Start by creating a daily or weekly schedule. Include school hours, extracurricular activities, study time, and free time. Having a structured routine makes it easier to allocate time for each task.

4. **Use a Planner or Organizer:**

   It's important to have a physical planner or digital organizer to jot down assignments, appointments, and activities. This tool can serve as a visual reminder and keep you on track.

5. **Avoid Procrastination:**

   There is a deep-rooted danger of procrastination that has been known to lead to stress and poor performance. By going at challenging tasks head on has its rewards.

6. **Break Down Tasks into Smaller Steps:**

   If a task seems overwhelming, you can always break it down into smaller, manageable steps. Completing these smaller tasks will give you a sense of progress and achievement. Also alleviate anxiety.

7. **Limit Distractions:**

   First you must identify common distractions, such as social media, video games, TV, and set specific times for leisure activities. During study or work time, keep distractions at bay. This is what champions do.

8. **Learn to Say No:**

   It's ok to say no! Understand the importance of saying no to commitments that might overload your schedule. It's okay to decline some invitations or activities if you have other obligations. This does not make you a bad person.

9. **Be Realistic:**

    Always set realistic expectations. If you never ran 10 miles don't wake up and say I'm going to run 10 miles today. Begin with, I'm going to run 2 miles today, 5 miles in 3 weeks, 10 miles next month. This will keep you from feeling down when you do not live up to an unrealistic, impulsive goal. Avoid overcommitting to avoid feeling overwhelmed and burned out.

10. **Take Breaks:**

    Emphasize the importance of taking short breaks during study or work sessions. Short breaks can help rejuvenate the mind and improve focus.

11. **Review and Adjust:**

    Regularly review your time management practices and make adjustments as needed. A flexible approach will allow you to fine-tune your schedule and strategies over time.

12. **Model Good Time Management:** *[Adults to Adolescents]*

    As parents, teachers and mentors, be a role model for effective time management. Let's show the next generation how to manage time and deal with daily tasks and responsibilities. Students ask your teachers or parents to give you an example.

Remember developing time management skills is a gradual process, and you will need guidance and support along the way. Remain patient and celebrate your progress.

Venetia, South Africa has more than 101 million carts of diamond reserves. China is the largest producer of Gold. Russia produces 74,000 metric tons of Palladium. All of these are precious commodities that come with appreciation in value. However, there is one commodity that is more precious than the three combined: *TIME!*

Time is valuable and cannot be replaced. It is a finite resource that cannot be regained once it's gone. Managing and prioritizing your time effectively can greatly impact your productivity, accomplishments, and overall quality of life.

Two statements often used:

1) 'Don't waste my time!'

2) 'Stop wasting time!'

Time is your most precious commodity!

Chapter 5

Goals & Vision

Setting goals and having a vision in high school is crucial for personal development and future success. As a teenager high school is a formative period where you will begin to explore different interests, skills, and passions. By setting goals and having a clear vision, will teach you how to focus on effort, build resilience, and work towards achieving aspirations. Here are some steps to help you while in high school set goals and create a vision for your future:

1. **Self-Reflection:**
   Always take some time for self-reflection. This will help identify strengths, weaknesses, interests, and values. Understanding yourself better will provide a foundation for setting meaningful goals. *(As this generation would say, facts!)*

2. **Short-term and Long-term Goals:**
   It is imperative to learn the importance of setting both short-term and long-term goals. Short-term goals can be achievable within a few weeks or months, while long-term goals can span several years. Make sure the goals are specific, measurable, achievable, relevant, and time-bound. *(Smart)*

3. **Academic Goals:**
   Academic success is a significant aspect of your life during high school. Set academic goals, such as achieving a certain GPA, getting involved in specific extracurricular activities, and taking advanced courses in subjects you enjoy. Why not learn on a collegian level in high school if you are able.

4. **Career Exploration:**
   It is very important to explore different careers and industries that align with 'your' interests and talents. This exploration can involve research, learning how to interview, internships, and shadowing professionals.

5. **Personal Development Goals:**
   Setting personal goals can help you improve various aspects of your life at an early age. These goals include becoming more organized, and learning good communication skills. This is crucial for building a strong foundation for your future.

6. **Health and Well-being:**
   This is extremely important to the Middie Mindset. With all of the pressures in today's social pressured *society,* it is very important that you pay close attention to your physical and mental well-being. Set goals related to regular exercise, healthy eating habits, stress management, and getting enough sleep. *(Highly Important Segment.)*

7. **Social Goals:**
   High school is a time for building friendships and social skills. Joining clubs, sports teams, positive organizations, promotes strong communication skills and a overall fun high school experience.

   The one who makes new friends, builds a new castle. –G, Mack.

8. **Community Involvement:**
   Learn to love to be socially involved within the student body of your school. This will spear into involvement within your community outside of school. Community service is a dope way to give back to society.

9. **Vision Board:**
   Creating a vision board can be a fun and creative way for you to visualize your goals and aspirations. It can include images, quotes, and symbols that represent your dreams and aspirations. There is insurmountable joy in being able to look back 5, 10 years from inception and being able to see what you envisioned before bringing it to life.

10. **Flexibility and Adaptability:**
    Lets understand that goals may change over time, and that's okay. These are important traits that will allow you to adjust to changing circumstances, learn new skills, and thrive in various situations. Being flexible means being open to different

approaches or ideas, while adaptability involves being able to modify your behavior, thinking, or plans to suit new circumstances. These qualities are particularly valuable in today's rapidly changing world, as they will enable you to navigate uncertainties and embrace opportunities more effectively. High-level essential qualities to own as life's circumstances and interests can evolve. *(Heat!)*

11. **Encouragement and Support:**
Be a supportive friend to peers as you all work towards this thing called winning. Offer encouragement, celebrate each other's achievements, and provide guidance during challenging times.

**Note: Owning a Middie Mindset will never allow you to tell someone who is trying, that they are no good. Aka, 'you suck', or 'you're trash.'* No, it's more like:

- Let's go! you got this!
- You're amazing.
- You can and you will.
- You are dope!

12. **Monitoring Progress:**
Keep notes and track your progress regularly. This self-assessment will help you stay on track and make adjustments as needed. For example: Day 1, Day 2. Week 1, Week 2. Month 1, Month 2.

13. **Resilience and Perseverance:**
High school life can be a rollercoaster ride with highs and lows. To thrive in this dynamic environment, you will need resilience – the ability to bounce back from adversity stronger than ever. Life is no sprint. It's a marathon. There is a profound amount of resilience and perseverance you must obtain to run your race. *(Run to your Burger King.)*

Guess what? Setbacks are real and in some cases inevitable. But never lose heart. Simply learn from them and keep pressing towards your goals. Always tell yourself, I am able!

Time For Some Chapter Notes:

5 Goals That You Would Like To Achieve Before Graduation:

1.

2.

3. ____
____
____

4. ____
____
____

5. ____
____
____

5 Goals You Would Like To Achieve By Age 21

1) ____
2) ____
3) ____
4) ____
5) ____

Remember that the goals and vision you set for yourself should be based on your passions and aspirations, not solely on external expectations. As a mentor and a person who believes in optimism I encourage you to dream big! Surround yourself with like-minded peers who are supportive and feel empowered to pursue their goals with confidence and determination.

Goal driven energy is transferrable. –G, Mack

Chapter 6

The Art of Self-Advocacy

The Art of Self-Advocacy –means that there is a great skill in doing that thing. Executing well what one has devised.

Self-advocacy is the empowering process of speaking up for your own rights, needs, and preferences. It involves effectively communicating your thoughts and concerns to others, ensuring your voice is heard and respected. By mastering self-advocacy, you can navigate challenges, make informed decisions, and actively shape your own experiences and outcomes. **Highly Important to the Middie Mindset.*

High school is not only about learning from textbooks but also about learning to speak up for yourself. This chapter will teach you the art of self-advocacy – how to communicate your needs effectively, seek help when necessary, and build strong relationships with peers, teachers, and mentors.

Throughout the journey of life we all have to live by rules. Some rules are enforced by Governments, States, and Municipalities. Then there are rules enforced by you. Rules in which are put in place to govern oneself. Nevertheless, they have to be enforced. My question to you, are you willing?

1. **Know Yourself:** Understand your strengths, weaknesses, interests, and learning style. This self-awareness will help you communicate your needs effectively. Knowing yourself is the beginning of all wisdom. **Know God First. Proverbs 9:10*

2. **Set Goals:** Clearly define your academic, personal, and social goals. Break them down into manageable steps to track your progress. It behooves you to keep it *'a hundred'* with yourself when setting goals. Goals are achieved in intervals.

3. **Effective Communication:** Learn to express your thoughts, needs, and concerns clearly and respectfully. Practice active listening to understand others as well. Your voice is your connection to the world of opportunity. It will enable a clear conveyance of ideas, reduce misunderstandings and strengthen relationship whether in personal, professional or social contexts.

4. **Seek Information:** Research and gather information about your rights, available resources, and support systems both within and outside of school. **Information seekers are rock stars!** They search the earth until they get the answers to all of their questions. How lucky are you that you are living in the information age. During my high school tenor, 1992-95 we did not have the luxury of the world-wide-web. Therefore you are left without any excuse. Maximize on the luxury of having infinite information in the palms of your hands.

5. **Speak Up:** Do not, *(I repeat)* Do not be afraid to ask questions, seek clarification, or voice concerns when necessary. Advocate for accommodations or modifications if they can help you succeed.
   An open mouth will soon prepare before you a buffet. –G , Mack.

6. **Build Relationships:** Cultivate positive relationships with teachers, counselors, and peers. Networking can provide valuable support and guidance. Strong relationships can lead to better collaborations, support networks and other opportunities for growth. Building your power circle takes time and effort, but the benefits can be far-reaching and conducive to your maturation.

7. **Problem-Solving:** As a high school student it is imperative to develop this attribute. It will force you to rely on

independence, creative thinking and critical thinking all in which will enhance a sense of readiness. In the moment being able to figure it out. This will enable you to identify and exploit opportunities in different environments. Who are problem solvers? People who think of new ideas, better ways of doing things. They make it easier for people to understand. They save time and money.

For every problem there is an answer. Empty your thoughts and allow the solution to visit you. -W, Isdom

8. **Build Confidence:** Believe in your abilities and the value of your perspective. Confidence empowers you to advocate for yourself effectively. Building confidence involves a combination of self-awareness, positive self-talk, setting achievable goals, embracing failures as learning opportunities, and engaging in activities you enjoy. Work at developing different skills, trying new things, and surrounding yourself with supportive peers will help boost your self-esteem over time.

9. **Persistence:** Don't give up easily. Let's repeat that. Don't give up easily! If you encounter obstacles, keep pushing forward and exploring different approaches to achieve your goals. Every champion at one point of time felt like quitting, throwing in the towel. But great is the reward for those who go the extra mile and give it their all. Always finish what you start. **Michael Jordan got cut from the high school basketball team. Tom Brady was selected 199 in the sixth round.*

10. **Stay Informed:** Stay updated on educational policies, changes, and opportunities that might impact your learning experience. Stay engaged in meaningful conversation. It will broaden your understanding of current events, cultivate critical thinking skills, and prepare you for a fast evolving society. Informed students are better equipped to navigate the world around them and contribute positively to their communities.

11. **Practice Self-Care:** Prioritize your well-being! Adequate sleep,

nutrition, and relaxation contribute to your overall success. Self- care is vital as it promotes your overall well-being and mental health. Adolescence can be a challenging period, marked by academic pressures, social changes, and emotional growth. Engaging in self-care activities like getting enough sleep. Practicing mindfulness, exercising and pursuing hobbies helps reduce stress, improves emotional resilience, and fosters a positive self-image. It is extremely important to remain hyper-focused on self-care as it manages stress. It is not often that I will advise you to be in a hurry, howbeit; I'm requesting that you stay in a hurry to build healthy habits that will help you develop the necessary skills for maintaining your well-being throughout your life span.

We cannot direct the wind, but we can adjust the sails. –D, Parton

Remember, Self-Advocacy is a skill that takes time to develop. Start small, and with practice you will become better at advocating for your needs and achieving your goals. *"Let's Grow!"*

Here is a short story that sheds light on what the Art of Self-Advocacy looks like in a high school setting.

Finding My Voice

Day 1

A Whisper in the Crowd

In the noisy hallways of Middlebrook High School, Sarah found herself fading into the background, her voice lost among the noise of classmates. Always a quiet and introspective teenager, she struggled to advocate for herself, both in and out of the classroom. Her friends seemed to effortlessly express their opinions, while Sarah remained unsure and hesitant.

Day 5

Unlikely Encounters

One day as Sarah sat alone in the school study area, she noticed a poster for the upcoming debate club tryouts. Intrigued, she decided to give it a shot. With every practice session, she found herself slowly shedding her inhibitions. Through rigorous preparation and guidance from her coach, Mr. Thompson, Sarah discovered the power of articulating her thoughts and defending her stance.

Day 20

Speaking Up Beyond the Classroom

As Sarah gained confidence within the debate club, she began to translate her newfound skills into her daily life. She started expressing her opinions in group projects, advocating for her preferences, and even sharing her ideas during class discussions. Her classmates were surprised by the transformation, and Sarah felt a sense of empowerment she had never experienced before.

Day 35

Confronting Challenges

However, self-advocacy was not without its challenges. Sarah faced moments of self-doubt and anxiety, but she refused to let them hold her back. With the support of her friends, family, and the skills she acquired in the debate club, she pushed through the barriers that once held her voice captive.

Day 60

A Voice Amplified

Sarah's journey culminated in the annual school debate

championship. The topic was "The Importance of Youth Voices in Decision-Making." Sarah's heartfelt and passionate argument left the audience in awe. Though she didn't win the competition, she had already won the battle within herself.

The End,

Epilogue

A Continued Journey

As Sarah continued her education and journey into adulthood, she carried the lessons of self-advocacy with her. She pursued her dreams with determination, unafraid to share her thoughts and make her presence known. Sarah's struggle had transformed into a strength, a beacon of hope for other teenagers navigating the challenges of finding their own voices.

Remember, self-advocacy is a journey, and just like Sarah, you have the power to overcome some obstacles and find your voice.

"we who have means and a voice must use them to help those who have neither."—J. Donnelly

Chapter 7

The Power of Active Listening

In a world buzzing with constant distractions and fast-paced interactions, the art of active listening holds a special significance for teenagers. This communication skill, often overlooked, possesses the potential to transform the way young minds navigate their relationships, education, and personal growth. *I wish I had this powerful tool offered to me at an earlier age.*

A. **Understanding Active Listening:** Active listening goes beyond merely hearing words; it involves fully engaging with the speaker's message. It requires setting aside one's own thoughts and distractions to focus entirely on what the speaker is saying. By giving undivided attention, you can decode both verbal and nonverbal cues, gaining a deeper understanding of the speaker's emotions, concerns, and perspectives.

B. **Building Stronger Relationships:** In a phase of life marked by forming new friendships active listening can be a powerful tool. When you actively listen, you will create an environment of trust and empathy. Friends and peers feel valued and understood, which in turn strengthens bonds and create healthier connections. By practicing active listening, you learn to put yourself in others shoes, leading to more meaningful relationships.

C. **Enhancing Academic Success:** Active listening is not limited to social interactions; it extends to the classroom as well. By intently focusing on teachers and peers during lectures and discussions, young minds absorb information more effectively. This skill enables you to grasp concepts, ask relevant questions, and engage in discussions that enhance your learning experience. As a result, active listening can positively impact academic performance and pave the way for a successful educational journey.

D. **Rational Listening:** It is given that you will face challenges and conflicts that require careful consideration and effective communication. Active listening plays a crucial role in conflict resolution and problem solving. By actively listening to opposing viewpoints and seeking to understand various perspectives it becomes easier to identify common ground and work toward solutions that benefit everyone involved. When rationalizing through listening you are able to generate your desired outcome, versus the undesired.

E. **Boosting Self-Confidence:** Active listening isn't just about focusing on others; it also involves acknowledging one's thoughts and emotions. By being present in the moment and practicing self-awareness, you will set the stage to better understand your own feelings and reactions. This happens when actively listening to your positive self-talk. This self-awareness, in turn, contributes to improved self-confidence and emotional intelligence. *(Fire!)*

F. **Cultivating Empathy and Tolerance:** You are now at a stage of life where you are learning about the diversity of the world and encountering various belief systems and cultures. Active listening helps to develop empathy and tolerance by encouraging an open-minded approach to different viewpoints. By truly listening to others it will broaden your horizons and develop a greater appreciation for the richness of human experience.

Now that we have scratched the surface of The Power of Active Listening, I would like for you to carefully absorb the study guide as you begin mastering this art. God has given us two ears and one mouth. I cannot express it enough that the one who becomes a great listener will obtain more knowledge than he or she could ever ask for. In return this will set you up for a sure win in life.

Study Guide

Active Listening For The Middie Mindset

Active listening is a crucial skill that helps you connect with others, improve communication, and build stronger relationships. Here is a study guide to help you develop effective active listening skills:

1. **Understanding Active Listening:**

   - Active listening is more than just hearing words; it involves focusing on the speaker, understanding their message, and responding appropriately.
   - It shows respect and empathy towards the speaker and makes them feel valued.

2. **Tips for Active Listening:**

   - **Maintain Eye Contact:** Look at the speaker to show that you're engaged and interested in what they're saying.
   - **Stay Attentive:** Avoid distractions like your phone or other thoughts and give your full attention to the speaker.
   - **Avoid Interrupting:** Let the speaker finish before you respond, even if you disagree or have something to say.
   - **Show Nonverbal Cues:** Nodding, smiling, and using facial expressions can show that you're engaged in the conversation.

3. **Active Listening Techniques:**

   - **Reflective Listening:** Repeat or paraphrase what the speaker said to show that you understand and are paying attention.
   - **Clarifying Questions:** Ask questions to ensure you grasp the speaker's point and to encourage them to elaborate.
   - **Summarizing:** Occasionally summarize the main points of the conversation to demonstrate your understanding.

4. **Empathy and Validation:**

    - Try to put yourself in the speaker's shoes to understand their feelings and perspective.
    - Use phrases like, "I understand how you feel," or "that must have been tough," to show empathy.

5. **Avoid Judging or Advising:**

    - Don't jump to conclusions or offer solutions too quickly; sometimes people just need someone to listen without judgment.
    - Avoid saying things like "You should have done..." or "If I were you..." as it can make the speaker feel invalidated.

6. **Be Patient:**

    - Sometimes people might take time to express themselves fully. Give them the space and time they need.

7. **Practice, Practice, Practice:**

    - Active listening is a skill that improves with practice. Engage in conversations with friends, family, and teachers to hone your skills.

8. **Understand The Benefits:**

    - Improved relationships and understanding with others.
    - Better communication skills that can serve you in school, work, and personal life.
    - Enhanced problem-solving abilities due to better comprehension of information.

9. **Recognize Barriers:**

    - Distractions, preconceived notions, or personal

biases can hinder effective listening. Be aware of these barriers and work to overcome them.

10. **Seek Feedback:**

- Ask friends or family members for feedback on your active listening skills. Constructive criticism can help you improve.

Remember, active listening is not just about hearing words but about connecting on a deeper level. As a teenager, developing this skill will greatly benefit your relationships and overall communication abilities.

In conclusion, the power of active listening for teenagers cannot be overstated. This skill will equip you with the tools to build stronger relationships, excel academically, navigate challenges, and cultivate essential life skills. By honing the art of active listening, you are laying the foundation for a future marked by effective communication, empathy, and personal growth.

James 1:19 "Let every person be quick to hear, slow to speak,"

Chapter 8

Character Ethics

Have you ever looked into the mirror and judged your character? More than likely, probably not. As a teenager this was something I never did. Truth be told, I could care less. I just wanted to play sports, go to school to have fun and go to the mall on the weekend. Unbeknownst, now that I look back I did pick up some good ethics along the way. From my parents, siblings, grandparents, friends, pastors and many schoolteachers. Be that as it may, now that we are working towards molding your Middie Mindset, it is imperative that you learn what Character Ethics are now, rather than hoping that you pick up a few along the way.

Character Ethics refer to the moral qualities and values that shape an individual's behavior, decisions, and interactions with others. Developing strong character ethics is crucial for personal growth, building healthy relationships, and becoming responsible members of society. This study guide will provide you with insights into various aspects of character ethics and practical tips for cultivating positive traits.

Understanding Character Ethics

1. **What Are Character Ethics?**

    - A philosophical approach that focuses on developing moral character and virtues in order to make ethical decisions.
    - One who focuses on making fundamental decisions.

2. **Key Virtues and Traits**

- Exploring virtues like honesty, integrity, empathy, responsibility, humility, compassion, and courage.
- Understanding the significance of each virtue in different life situations.

Developing Character Ethics

1. **Self-Awareness and Reflection**:

- Pay close attention to your daily development.
- Practice self-reflection to identify strengths and areas for improvement.
- Know your weaknesses.

2. **Set Personal Goals**:

- Identify, then stand on it.
- Align your actions with your values to build strong character.
- Don't be easily moved. *(Uprooted)*

3. **Make Ethical Decisions:**

- Govern your decisions like a Supreme Court Judge.
- Memorize your top 5 core beliefs.
- Stand on your principles.
- Ethical decision-making models [e.g. SODA: Stop, Options, Decide, Act]

4. **Resisting Peer Pressure:**

- First Recognize the root of your surrounding peer pressures.

- Never compromise or allow it to contradict your core values.
- Create strategies for saying "no" while maintaining respectful relationships.

Applying Character Ethics

1. **Building Empathy:**

   - Examine your biases.
   - Ask the right questions.
   - Challenge prejudices and stereotypes.
   - Withhold judgment.

2. **Practicing Honesty:**

   - Admitting when you are wrong.
   - Choosing not to cheat.
   - A willingness to value real over being right. *(Heat!)*

3. **Demonstrating Integrity:**

   - Respect yourself and others no matter where you are.
   - Reliability and trustworthiness.
   - Loyalty and refusing to compromise on matters of principle.

4. **Exercising Responsibility**:

   - Showing up on time.
   - Taking responsibility for your actions and their consequences.
   - If you sign up, show up.

5. **Display Courage:**

   - Differentiating between physical and moral courage.
   - Overcoming fears and standing up for what is right.

- Face difficulties head-on.
- Challenge the status quo.

- **Types of Courage**

  a. **Physical courage** – Feeling fear yet choosing to act.
  b. **Emotional courage** – Following your heart.
  c. **Intellectual courage** – Expanding your horizons, letting go of the familiar.
  d. **Social courage** – To be yourself in the face of adversity.

Continuous Improvement

1. **Life Long Learning:**

   - Embracing a growth mindset for character development.
   - Seeking opportunities for learning and personal growth.

2. **Seeking Feedback:**

   - Importance of feedback in identifying areas for improvement.
   - Receiving and acting on constructive criticism.

3. **Role Models and Mentorship:**

   - Identifying positive role models and mentors.
   - Learning from their character traits and experiences.
   - *Know the difference in being Mislead vs Mentored.

Ten Reasons Why Character Ethics Are Important For Teenager

1) **Moral Foundation:** Developing strong character ethics provides teenagers with a solid moral foundation that guides their decisions and actions in various situations.

2) **Decision-Making Skills:** Ethical principles help teenagers make thoughtful and responsible decisions, considering the impact of their choices regarding themselves and others.

3) **Empathy and Compassion:** Are not one-time actions, but ongoing attitudes and behaviors. Building these character ethics enables teenagers to build meaningful connections that positively impact their lives.

4) **Relationship Building:** High-principled behavior promotes healthy relationships based on trust, respect, and integrity. It helps by cultivating meaningful connections with peers, family and mentors.

5) **Conflict Resolution:** Teenagers with strong character ethics are more equipped to handle conflicts and disagreements in a constructive and fair manner, promoting peaceful resolutions.

6) **Self-Reflection:** Conscientious development encourages teenagers to reflect on their actions and values, fostering self-awareness and personal growth.

7) **Resilience:** Ethical values like perseverance and honesty help teenagers develop resilience, enabling them to overcome challenges and setbacks with determination.

8) **Long-Term Success:** Employers and educational institutions value individuals with strong character ethics, as they are more likely to exhibit professionalism, teamwork, and dedication.

9) **Community Contribution:** Ethical teenagers are more inclined to engage in community service and contribute to their surroundings, making a meaningful impact.

10) **Preparation for Adulthood:** Building character ethics during teenage years prepares individuals for adulthood by instilling principles that guide them through life's complexities.

Incorporating character ethics into your life is a journey that requires commitment and effort. By cultivating virtues like honesty, integrity, empathy, responsibility, and courage, you'll not only enhance your personal well-being but also contribute positively to your community. Remember that character development is an ongoing process, and every choice you make shapes the person you become.

Before closing out this chapter there is one last vital piece of information you are going to need to add to the growth of the Middie Mindset. 'Character Ethics' and 'Personality Ethics' are two different traits. So, rather than it being defined for you, it's time to put your brain to work. Or, shall we say Google to work. *(lol)*

Character Ethics Focuses On?

____

____

____

____

____

Personality Ethics Focuses On?

____

____

____

____

____

Character Ethics are the foundation for success. –G, Mack

Chapter 9

Cognitive Thinking

Imagine a world where you can unravel complex problems, make informed decisions, and adapt to new situations with ease. This world is within your grasp, thanks to the remarkable power of cognitive thinking. In this chapter, we will dive into what cognitive thinking is, why it matters, and how you can harness its potential to excel in both academics and everyday life.

First you must understand what Cognitive Thinking is. It refers to the mental process that allows you to gather, process, analyze, and interpret information from the world around us. It involves reasoning, problem-solving, decision-making, critical analysis, and creativity. In simple terms, cognitive thinking is about using your brain to think deeply and effectively. Sounds like cognitive thinking is a intricate part of molding the Middie Mindset.

Why Does Cognitive Thinking Matter

Cognitive thinking is like a mental toolkit that equips you to face challenges head-on. Whether you are solving a math problem, crafting an essay, or navigating social situations, cognitive thinking enables you to:

- **Solve Problems:** Tackling puzzles, riddles, and complex equations becomes more manageable when you apply cognitive thinking. It helps break down large problems into smaller, solvable parts.

- **Make Informed Decisions:** From choosing a career path to deciding what to eat for lunch, cognitive thinking aids in evaluating options, considering consequences, and making choices that align with your goals.

- **Adapt to Change:** Life is full of unexpected twists. Cognitive thinking allows you to adapt to new situations, learn from experiences, and adjust your strategies accordingly.

- **Enhance Learning:** Engaging in cognitive thinking deepens your understanding of subjects. You connect ideas, see patterns, and remember concepts more effectively.

- **Promote Creativity:** Cognitive thinking encourages you to explore different perspectives, combine ideas, and come up with innovative solutions to problems.

How To Develop Cognitive Thinking Skills

- **Ask Questions:** Curiosity is the fuel for cognitive thinking. Do not be afraid to ask (***why, how,*** and ***what if***) questions. Seek to understand the underlying reasons and connections.

- **Practice Reflection:** Set aside time to reflect on your experiences. Consider what you have learned, how you could have approached things differently, and how you can apply these insights in the future.

- **Break Down Problems:** When faced with a challenge, break it down into smaller parts. Address each part methodically, and gradually piece together the solution.

- **Consider Alternatives:** Instead of settling for the first solution that comes to mind, explore multiple options. Evaluate their pros and cons, and choose the most suitable one.

- **Embrace Mistakes:** Mistakes are stepping-stones to growth. Analyze your mistakes, understand what went wrong, and use that knowledge to improve. *(It's ok to stumble.)*

- **Engage in Critical Thinking:** Analyze information critically by evaluating its reliability, credibility, and potential biases. Separate facts from opinions to make well-informed judgments.

A short story on how Cognitive Thinking can look in its truest from.

Corey's Cognition

Corey a quiet and introspective teenager, often found himself lost in thought amidst the fast pace of his high school. While others chatted and socialized, Corey's mind was a realm of deep contemplation and observation. He wasn't one to speak up often, but his cognitive thinking abilities were unparalleled.

One day, his school's art club faced a daunting challenge. They were tasked with creating a mural that would reflect the diversity and unity of the student body. As ideas flew around the room, Corey listened carefully and absorbed the various perspectives. While everyone seemed to be struggling to come up with a cohesive concept, Corey quietly started sketching.

Over the next few days, Corey spent his free periods sketching and refining his idea. He drew a tree with intricate, interconnected branches, each branch representing a different aspect of the student body, different cultures, interests, and backgrounds. He envisioned the leaves as vibrant colors, signifying unity in diversity.

When Corey finally unveiled his sketch to the art club, there was a hushed silence followed by awe-filled murmurs. The concept resonated deeply with everyone, capturing the essence of what they wanted to convey. With Corey's guidance, the mural came to life on a large wall of the school, becoming a symbol of harmony and acceptance.

Corey's cognitive thinking did not stop there. His quiet nature allowed him to truly listen and understand others. When friends came to him with personal problems, he offered thoughtful advice that helped them see their situations from new angles. He had a way of simplifying complex problems and presenting solutions that made people feel empowered.

As the years went by, Corey's cognitive thinking abilities continued to shape his path. He pursued a career in psychology, where his ability to analyze situations from multiple angles and empathize with others made him an exceptional therapist even in his quiet demeanor, Corey's impact was profound, as he helped countless individuals navigate the complexities of their lives.

Corey's story serves as a reminder that cognitive thinking doesn't always need to be loud or flashy. Sometimes, the quiet ones possess the power to see things in ways that others might overlook, leaving a lasting impact on those around them.

The End,

- Do you know a Corey?
- What part of Corey's Cognition can you relate to the most?
- How did Corey use his Cognitive Thinking to become the person he desired to be?

Putting Cognitive Thinking into Action

Whether you're preparing for a test, brainstorming a project, or making a life decision, cognitive thinking will be your guide. Remember, it is not about having all the answers, but about the process of thinking deeply and critically. Embrace challenges, seek diverse perspectives, and never stop asking questions. By developing your cognitive thinking skills, you are equipping yourself to thrive in a world that values innovation, adaptability, and informed decision-making.

In the next chapter, explore the fascinating world of problem-solving strategies that can elevate your cognitive thinking to new heights. Stay curious and keep thinking.

One of life's more beautiful challenges is to think. –G, Mack.

Chapter 10

Problem Solving

Problem solving is a valuable skill that empowers individuals to tackle challenges, make informed decisions, and innovate. Developing strong problem-solving skills during high school sets the foundation for success in academics, careers, relationships, and everyday life.

Problem Solving For Teenagers

1. **Understand the Problem:**

    - Read the problem carefully and identify the key components.
    - Define the problem in your own words to ensure a clear understanding.

2. **Break Down the Problem:**

    - Divide complex problems into smaller, manageable parts.
    - Create a step-by-step plan to address each part.

3. **Gather Information:**

    - Research and gather relevant information to better understand the problem.
    - Consult textbooks, online resources, and experts if necessary.

4. **Analyze the Situation:**

    - Identify patterns, trends, and relationships within the information.
    - Consider different perspectives to gain a comprehensive view.

5. **Generate Solutions:**

    - Brainstorm multiple solutions, even if some seem unconventional.
    - Encourage creative thinking and don't dismiss ideas prematurely.

6. **Evaluate Options:**

    - Assess the pros and cons of each solution.
    - Consider potential outcomes, feasibility, and ethical implications.

7. **Choose the Best Solution:**

    - Select the solution that aligns with your goals and values.
    - Trust your judgment but remain open to feedback.

8. **Implement the Solution:**

    - Execute your chosen solution using your action plan. Become the solution.
    - Adjust your approach as needed based on real-world feedback.

9. **Reflect and Learn:**

    - After implementing the solution, reflect on the results.
    - Analyze what worked well and what could be improved.

10. **Iterate and Adapt:**

    - If the solution isn't entirely successful, don't be discouraged. Pause, practice more until adapting and improving.
    - There is no such thing as one-size fits all when it comes to research. But there are: objectives, questions, hypotheses, resources and even risk on the road to figuring it out. *(Big Facts)*

11. **Practice Regularly:**

    - Regularly engage in various types of problems to build diverse problem-solving skills.
    - Practice reinforces your abilities and enhances your confidence. No one person in a successful position got there with out practicing first. *(Remember Shortcuts.)*

12. **Collaborate and Seek Help:**

    - Don't hesitate to seek help or collaborate with peers.
    - Different perspectives can lead to more robust solutions.

13. **Stay Patient and Persistent:**

    - Complex problems may take time to solve—persevere and remain patient.
    - Persistence is key to overcoming challenges.

14. **Learn from Failure:**

    - Embrace failures as opportunities for growth and learning.
    - Analyze what went wrong and how to avoid similar mistakes.

15. **Apply Problem Solving Everywhere:**

- Use problem-solving skills in academics, personal life, sports participation and when seeing anything that could use a solvent.
- The ability to solve problems is highly transferrable.

Note Why:

___
___
___
___
___

Problem solving is an essential skill that empowers high school students to navigate challenges and create meaningful solutions. By mastering the Art of Problem solving you will set yourself up for success in both the academic journey and future endeavors.

Steve Jobs Three-Step Method To Solving Difficult Problems:

1. **Zoom Out:** Difficult problems involve difficult-to-find solutions.
2. **Focus In:** Once you know what you are looking for, give yourself a period of intense thinking and fact gathering.
3. **Disconnect:** Take a break. Walk, exercise, relax.

Why do you think problem solving is important as a teenager?

___
___
___
___
___
___
___

It takes a village to come up with solutions, but a good problem solver can steer the team towards the best choices and implement strategies to achieve the desired result.

Chapter 11

Outwitting Social Pressure

High school years are a time of self-discovery, growth, and countless new experiences. Amidst this exciting journey, teenagers often find themselves navigating through a complex web of social pressures that can sometimes feel overwhelming. From fitting in with peer groups to adhering to societal expectations, the challenges posed by these pressures can impact both mental and emotional well-being. In this chapter, we will delve into the various aspects of social pressure that high school teenagers encounter, offering insights and strategies to help you, *the teenager,* confidently navigate this intricate terrain while staying true to yourself or as this generation would say, *'keeping it a hundred.'* By understanding the nature of social pressures and learning how to make informed decisions allows you to stay locked in and forever knowing that you can forge your own path. This permits you to create healthy relationships, and develop the resilience needed to flourish during these transformative years. *Let's Grow!*

What Is Social Pressure

Social pressure refers to the influence that others have on our thoughts, feelings, behaviors, and decisions. It is the tendency for individuals to conform to the norms and expectations of their social group in order to fit in, gain approval, or avoid disapproval. Social pressure can come from family, friends, peers, society, or even media. It can lead people to adopt beliefs or behaviors they might not necessarily agree with in order to avoid isolation or criticism.

OMG! How many of you have suffered from wanting to fit in, gain others approval to avoid disapproval? I'll be the first to admit, I'm guilty. I believe around 13 years of age I developed my own thinking wave. However, at some point all of us who have walked this planet have fell victim to Social Pressure. As the author of this book, 46 years of age, just last year I gave in to Social Pressure.

In the year of 2001 I came up with a slogan for Adidas. 'All Day I Dream About Surviving. *SDV,* short for Survivors Division. Now being a Leukemia survivor it seems as if the brand was tailored for me. Without hesitation I gave up the swoosh, *Nike.*

For years I would walk into shoes stores and see the dopest pair of Nikes, Jordans and other signature designs and simply shrug my shoulders and proceed to the Adidas section. So here comes late 2021. I'm constantly seeing friends at social gatherings wearing Jordan 1's. I look online, Jordan 1's. Attending high school basketball games and all I'm seeing is Jordan 1's. One day as I joked with a 6th grade player I was coaching, I asked him to ask his dad if I could barrow a pair of his Jordan 1's. Really I was joking with the kid, or was I?

Nearly a month later I landed at a shoe store to purchase some Yeezy's. Just below sat a pair of Jordan 1's. Normally I would shrug my shoulder and stick to the plan. However this day something different happened. Without reservation my hand picked up the Jordan shoe and began to take observation of it. I thought about everyone I had been seeing wear them. In a strange way I felt left out. I started hearing the complements. "Nice Shoes." But why? I'm comfortable with the shoes I've been wearing. *But they don't clean up like Jordan 1's,* was my self-talk. Before long I tried them on and days later I had them on at a social event. "I like them Jordan 1's," some stated. It was then that I realized what had happened.

So here we have a snap shot of how even us adults who understand thinking errors, case studies, dos and don'ts can still fall into the grasps of social pressure.

Social Pressure can also be part of the implicit demands that our culture or society weigh on us with the expectation that we will conform to in certain ways.

Learning Social Pressure

1. **Conformity:** Often feeling pressured to conform to social norms and fit in with peers to avoid standing out or being isolated.

2. **Peer Acceptance:** The desire to be accepted by friends and peers can lead you to make choices you wouldn't otherwise make just to gain approval.

3. **Body Image:** Media portrayal of ideal body types can lead to body dissatisfaction and unhealthy behaviors such as extreme dieting or excessive exercise.

4. **Material Possessions:** The need to own certain brands or items can arise from the desire to be seen as successful or cool by peers.

5. **Academic Performance:** Pressure to excel academically can come from parents, teachers, and classmates, leading to stress and unhealthy study habits.

6. **Online Presence:** You may feel pressure to maintain a curated online persona that reflects popularity and perfection, even if it doesn't match reality.

7. **Risk-Taking Behavior:** To fit in, you could be asked to take part in risky behaviors like experimenting with drugs or alcohol, or engaging in other dangerous activities.

8. **Relationships:** Influenced in choice of friendships and romantic relationships, potentially leading to unhealthy connections.

9. **Fear of Missing Out** (FOMO): The fear of missing out on social events or experiences can cause teens to participate in activities they are not comfortable with.

10. **Cultural and Ethnic Pressure:** Cultural or ethnic expectations can lead to feelings of pressure to conform to

certain traditions or norms within your community.

11. **Decision Making:** You may struggle with decision-making, feeling pressured to make choices that align with your friends' decisions rather than your own values.

12. **Social Media Comparison:** Constant exposure to others' seemingly perfect lives on social media can lead to feelings of inadequacy and pressure to measure up.

13. **Independence vs. Conformity**: Balancing the desire for independence with the pressure to conform to peer expectations can be challenging for teenagers, adults too.

14. **Mental Health Impact:** The cumulative effects of social pressure can contribute to stress, anxiety, and low self-esteem.

**Be careful to pay close attention to these signs.*

Can you identify the times when you were suffered by any of the listed pressures.

Notes:

____

____

____

____

____

Social Pressure Turned Peer

A. Spoken Peer Pressure:

Spoken peer pressure is when a teenager asks, suggests, persuades, or otherwise directs another to engage in a specific behavior. If this is done in a one-on-one environment, the recipient of the influence has a stronger chance of adhering to his or her core values and beliefs. If, however, the spoken influence takes place within a group, the pressure to go along with the group is immense.

B. Unspoken Peer Pressure:

With unspoken peer pressure a teenager is exposed to the actions of one or more peers and is left to choose whether they want to follow along. This could take the form of fashion choices, personal interactions or 'joining' types of behavior, (clubs, cliques, teams, etc.). Many young teens lack the mental maturity to control impulses and make wise long-term decisions. Because of this, many teens are more susceptible to influence from older or more popular friends.

C. Direct Peer Pressure:

This type of peer pressure can be spoken or unspoken. Direct peer pressure is normally behavior-centric. Examples of these kinds of behavior would be when a teenager hands another teen an alcoholic drink, or makes a sexual advance, or looks at another student's paper during a test. The other teen is put in a position of having to make an on-the-spot decision.

D. Indirect Peer Pressure:

Similar to unspoken peer pressure, indirect peer pressure is subtle but can still exert a strong influence on an impressionable young person. When a teen overhears a friend gossiping about another person and then reacts to the gossip that is indirect peer pressure. Or if a middle school student learns that the popular kids' parties include alcohol or drugs, that indirect pressure may prompt them to experiment as a way to gain acceptance.

E. Negative Peer Pressure:

Asking a young teenager to engage in behavior that is against their moral code or family values is a type of negative peer pressure. Teens see the actions of other teens with stronger personalities and are put in a position of following the leader or walking away. It's not uncommon for teens with strong morals to find themselves engaging in behavior that goes against their beliefs, simply because they want acceptance. Young people often lack the skills to come up with an excuse or reason to say no to negative peer pressure.

E. Positive Peer Pressure:

A group dynamic can be a positive peer influence if the behaviors are healthy, age-appropriate, and socially acceptable. For instance, if a peer group wants to make good grades, a young teen can be positively influenced to study. Or if a popular friend wants to earn money and save to buy a car, a less outgoing teenager may also be influenced to get a job and open a savings account. If members of the football team take a pledge to abstain from drinking alcohol to focus on staying healthy and having a winning season, other students may adopt the same behavior.

Frankly, it is going to be nearly impossible to go through high school and escape peer pressure. However, you now have this manual to learn from. I wish this road map leading to a growth mindset was handed to me while in High School. *To know means to soon be!* I was clueless to Social Pressure. No one touched on this subject throughout my 4-year high school tenor. But you, you on the other hand are now without excuse once you take ownership of this book. Obtaining the knowledge is the first step. You got this! I am cheering for you. Moreover, remember to stay true to self, focus on your interests, and surround yourself with supportive friends. Never be afraid to say 'NO' if something does not align with your core values and belief system. It is okay to be different and make your own choices. That is what makes you dope!

Knowing will make your wise decisions, ignorance will follow social pressure. –G, Mack

Chapter 12

Emotional Fitness

Ok, let's just come right out and say it. **It's ok, to not be ok!** *Exhale.* What does that mean? It means to be at a point where you are emotionally fatigued. Again, it's ok. To be human is to one day become emotionally fatigued. If this never happens to you then we have a problem, a very serious problem because this means you are from Mars. *(LoL.)*

In this chapter we are going to go over what it takes to become emotionally fit. The same way you train your body to become fit, is the same way you have to train your emotions, which is a very important piece to your overall well-being. It involves being able to recognize, express, and manage your feelings without becoming overwhelmed or out of control. Emotional Fitness is also closely related to mental health, which also includes having positive relationships with others and being able to cope with stressful situations that arise from time to time. However, Emotional Fitness focuses more on managing feelings and emotions, while mental health focuses more on cognitive functioning.

What Are Emotions

Emotions are complex psychological and physiological responses to stimuli, experiences, or thoughts. They often involve feelings such as happiness, sadness, anger, fear, and love. Emotions can influence our behavior, thoughts, and decision-making, playing a crucial role in human interactions and overall well-being.

Now that we understand what emotions are let's hone in on the key statement within the definition. Emotions can 'INFLUENCE' our behavior, thoughts, and decision-making. Pay close attention to what you just read. So not only do we have outside influences, we also possess an internal influencer aside from our standard conscious and unconscious decision maker called emotions. So how do you begin to know and understand this alter ego, persuader so you have it?

Understanding Emotions

Your high school years will mark a period of significant growth and change as you approach adulthood. Understanding emotions is a crucial development during this time. Your decision-making is depending on you to lock in and add this into your mental weaponry so that when the time comes, and it will, your Middie Mindset will automatically kick in and assist you.

Emotional Regulation Strategies

1. **Identify Emotions:**

    - Recognize and name your emotions accurately. *See Frequency Chart on Page 64.*
    - Use emotion words to express how you feel.

---

2. **Mindfulness Practice:**

    - Develop mindfulness techniques like deep breathing and meditation.
    - Focus on the present moment to manage overwhelming emotions.

3. **Healthy Coping Mechanisms**:

    - Develop positive ways to cope with stress, such as engaging in hobbies, exercising, or spending time with loved ones.
    - Block all unhealthy coping strategies like self-harm or substance use.

Current Unhealthy List:

___

___

___

___

4. **Pause and Reflect:**

    - Before it happens, take a moment before reacting impulsively. (*Very Important.)*
    - Always consider the consequences of your actions.

5. **Journaling:**

    - Keep a journal to express your feeling and thoughts. It is a healthy way to vent.
    - A journal will help you process emotions and gain insights into your triggers. *Vital*

6. **Social Support:**

    - Never allow yourself to feel alone. Keep the communication line open to friends, family, and mentors when feeling overwhelmed.
    - Discussing emotions with others can provide comfort and perspective. Find 1-3 people who you feel you can share anything with, and trust. (*Highly Important.)*

7. **Self-Care:**

- It is highly significant to focus on self-care activities like taking breaks, getting enough sleep, eating healthy, and meditation.
- Keep up with physicals, and form a healthy routine.

8. **Positive Self-Talk:**

- Challenge negative thoughts and replace them with positive affirmations: **I am dope! I am beautiful! I am smart!**
- You become the positive voice in negative moments!!!

9. **Setting Boundaries:**

- Assertively communicate your limits and say no when needed. (*Moxie)*
- Setting boundaries can reduce feelings of being overwhelmed.

10. **Distraction Techniques:**

- Practice engaging in activities that divert your attention from distressing emotions.
- Listening to music, watching a movie, working out or pursuing a new hobby. Taking a walk with a friend.

11. **Seeking Professional Help:**

- If emotional regulation becomes challenging, it is ok seeking support from a therapist or counselor.
- Can provide specialized guidance and strategies that parents, teachers, or friends may not be able to.

12. **Practice Empathy:**

- It is very important to stop and listen in order to

understand others' perspectives and feelings.

- Developing empathy can improve your emotional understanding and interpersonal skills.
- Pay close attention to others words, body language and feelings.

13. **Gratitude Practice:**

- I am advising that you keep a gratitude journal to focus on positive aspects of life.
- Gratitude can enhance overall emotional well-being. Having an appreciation to all things, big or small will shape you into a beautiful and well-in-tune person.

The more grateful I am, the more beauty I see. –Mary Davis

I am thankful for:

____

____

____

____

____

____

____

____

____

____

____

____

____

Visualize Calmness:

A. Visualization exercises is a great way to imagine or be in a peaceful place as you physically decompress.
B. Visualization can provide a sense of calm during stressful moments. Find peaceful places out in nature.

By equipping yourself with these emotional regulation strategies, you will soon develop resilience, learn to cope with challenges, and build healthier relationships with yourself and others. Practicing these techniques is a sure way to balancing your Emotional Fitness and overall life satisfaction.

Factors Affecting Emotional Understanding

1. **Cognitive Development:** High school students' cognitive abilities will continue to mature, enabling them to analyze and label their emotions more accurately. Their expanding vocabulary and abstract thinking skills contribute to a deeper comprehension of complex feelings.

2. **Peer Interactions:** Peer relationships are central to emotional development. High school students learn from their interactions with friends, experiencing a range of emotions in different social contexts. These interactions provide opportunities for empathy, conflict resolution, and emotional expression.

3. **Academic Stress:** The demands of high school academics can trigger various emotions, from achievement-related pride to anxiety and frustration. Understanding these emotions helps to manage stress and academic pressures more effectively.

4. **Family Dynamics:** The family environment remains influential in emotional understanding. Adolescents who communicate openly with their families about emotions tend to

develop stronger emotional intelligence. Family support also impacts how students perceive and manage their feelings.

5. **Media Exposure:** High school students are exposed to a wide array of emotions through media, including social media, movies, and music. Media can shape their emotional vocabulary and influence their understanding of complex emotional situations.

Implications and Benefits

- **Emotional Regulation:**

  High school students who grasp emotional understanding can better regulate their own emotions. This skill is vital for managing stress, making decisions, and maintaining mental well-being.

- **Interpersonal Relationships:**

  Emotional intelligence enhances communication and empathy, fostering healthier friendships and relationships. Students who understand their own emotions are more adept at recognizing and responding to others' feelings.

- **Academic Performance:**

  Emotional understanding contributes to better academic performance. Students can effectively manage the emotional challenges associated with exams, assignments, and social interactions.

Emotions, often considered abstract and intangible, can also be viewed through the lens of energy and vibration. As humans, we experience a wide spectrum of emotions throughout our lives, manifesting through physiological responses within our bodies. The biological aspect of emotions involves an intricate interplay among hormones, neurotransmitters, and the nervous system. Like everything else in the universe, these biological constituents are composed of atoms that vibrate and generate energy.

The journey of understanding emotions, as a high school student is intricate, influenced by cognitive, social, and personal factors. High school years are a critical period for developing emotional intelligence, which has far-reaching implications for an overall you, relationships, and future endeavors. Recognizing the importance of Emotional Fitness in this stage of your life will reveal the reward as you age.

As life goes on you will look back and thank yourself for tapping into the emotional side of you. We are all wired with various emotions. So as we bring this chapter to an end, I'll leave you with a list of emotions and their frequencies.

700+	Enlightenment
600	Peace
540	Joy
500	Love
400	Reason
350	Acceptance
310	Willingness
250	Neutrality
200	Courage
175	Pride
150	Anger
125	Desire
100	Fear
75	Grief
50	Apathy
30	Guilt
20	Shame

****Frequency of Emotions.*** Understand that some people may be operating at a lower frequency than you. This is your guide to understand that emotionally you may never be on the same frequency as others, which will allow you to tune them out as you remain on your high vibrating emotional frequency. Ultimately reaching the pinnacle of emotional fitness.

95% of decisions are made by how you feel in the moment. Manage your emotions.

Chapter 13

Go Getter

What Is A Go-Getter

A "Go-Getter" is a student who is proactive, self-motivated, and is willing to put in the effort required to overcome challenges. They have a strong work ethic, focus on continuous improvement, and are not afraid to step out of their comfort zone to seize opportunities. They seek elevation, personal growth, and take on leadership roles both inside and outside of the classroom. They believe in setting high standards, being adaptable, and maintaining a positive attitude even in the face of obstacles. A Go-Getter believes in taking the initiative, being persistent, and continuously pushing oneself beyond comfort zones to achieve success.

Being a teenage go-getter can bring many benefits. It allows you to develop strong work ethic, honesty, grit, passion, and a sense of accomplishment early on. Pursuing your goals with determination can lead to personal growth, better opportunities, and a head start on your future.

Let us take out some time to meet a high school Go-Getter.

'High School Hank'

A moment in time in the vibrant classrooms of Valley High School there lived a teenager named Hank who was known by all as 'High School Hank the Go-Getter.' Hank's determination and enthusiasm were infectious, inspiring his peers and teachers alike.

From his first day of high school, Hank set his sights on making the most of every opportunity. Raised by his grandparents in a household were ends were barely met, and facing the daily challenges of a poverty stricken community, Hank was always determined to grow up and become a difference maker. He had a notebook filled with his goals, dreams, and a detailed plan on how to achieve them. Never content with just attending classes; he actively engaged with teachers, asking questions, and always eager for additional resources to deepen his understanding. Everyone knew that there was something different about him.

Hank's go-getter attitude extended beyond academics. He joined the chess club, basketball team, theater and community service projects. He saw every club meeting as a chance to learn something new and every challenge as an opportunity to grow. Whether it was participating in the school's talent shows or taking on a leadership role as team captain, Hank was always up for a challenge.

One day, the school announced a prestigious public speaking competition. Hank knew this was his chance to shine. With no formal training he immediately began researching, practicing, and seeking guidance from his teachers and watching seasoned speakers on YouTube. He worked tirelessly on his speech, rehearsing in front of the mirror refining his delivery, and incorporating feedback, mainly from strangers. Though he put in tireless hours a small part of him felt he may not be good enough being that he was stepping into an unknown arena. He thought of all of his successful moments, but could not disregard all of the shortcomings. Being the go-getter he'd always been the words of his grandfather would always replay in his mind, *whenever in self-doubt, it's the go-getter who never learned to spell the word afraid.*

Soon the day of the competition arrived. Confidently Hank stepped onto the stage radiating from his every move. He delivered his speech flawlessly, captivating the audience with his words and passion. The judges were impressed not only by his content but also by his unwavering self-assuredness.

Hank won the competition, but for him, the real victory was in the journey. He had overcome doubts, pushed his limits, and turned a challenge into an opportunity for personal growth. His go-getter mindset had paid off, not just in the form of a trophy, but in the friendships he forged, the skills he developed, and the knowledge he gained.

As Hank's high school years came to a close, he reflected on the impact of his go-getter mentality. He had embraced every moment, turned setbacks into comebacks, and paved his own path to success. Graduating with a heart full of accomplishments and a mind eager for the future, High School Hank the Go-Getter left an indelible mark on Valley High School, inspiring others to seize life's opportunities with the same zest and determination.

As graduation approached, Hank's achievements did not go unnoticed. He was offered scholarships to prestigious universities, but he decided to attend a college that shared his passion for social justice and community service. During his high school years he planned to study political science, but eventually pursued a career in public service.

Hank's go-getter attitude and determination remained with him throughout his college years and beyond. He continued to excel academically while actively participating in organizations that made a positive impact on society. His hard work and dedication paid off when he was elected as the mayor of the City of Highview, the very town where his journey had begun. As mayor Hank implemented policies that addressed the needs of the community. He focused on improving education, creating job opportunities, and promoting community restorations.

His peers, who had witnessed his journey from high school to mayor, were not surprised by his accomplishments. They knew that *'High School Hank'* was destined for greatness. Hank's story serves as an inspiration to all those who encounter challenges in their lives. He teaches us that with determination, hard work, and a positive mindset, we can overcome any obstacle and achieve our dreams. He reminds us that it is never too early to make a difference and that our actions can have a profound impact on the world around us.

And it is so, the Go-Getter, high school student named Hank continued to make a difference, leaving an indelible mark on his community and inspiring generations to come.

The End,

Go-Getter Must Do List

- **Set Clear Goals:** Define both short-term and long-term goals for academics, extracurricular activities, personal development, and more.

- **Plan Ahead:** Use a planner or digital tool to organize tasks, assignments, and activities to stay on top of your commitments.

- **Take Initiative:** Don't wait for things to happen; actively seek out opportunities to learn, participate, and contribute.

- **Embrace Challenges:** See challenges as opportunities for growth. Approach difficult tasks with determination and a willingness to learn.

- **Manage Time Wisely:** Prioritize tasks, allocate time efficiently, and avoid procrastination to make the most of your day.

- **Stay Curious:** Cultivate a thirst for knowledge by exploring new subjects, reading books, and engaging in discussions.

- **Continuous Improvement:** Regularly assess your progress, identifying areas for improvement and adjusting your strategies accordingly.

- **Networking:** Build relationships with peers, mentors, and professionals to learn from their experiences and expand your horizons.

- **Positive Mindset:** Cultivate optimism and resilience. Focus on solutions rather than dwelling on problems.

- **Celebrate Wins:** Acknowledge your achievements, no matter how small, as they contribute to your overall progress.

- **Step Out of Comfort Zones:** Try new activities and experiences that challenge your limits and help you build confidence.

- **Learn from Failures:** Don't be afraid to make mistakes. Instead, use them as learning opportunities to refine your approach.

- **Practice Self-Care:** Prioritize your well-being through exercise, proper nutrition, adequate sleep, and relaxation.

- **Communicate Effectively:** Develop strong communication skills, both verbal and written, to express your ideas clearly and confidently.

- **Seek Feedback:** Be open to receiving feedback from peers, teachers, and mentors, using it to improve your skills and performance.

Remember, adopting a "Go-Getter" mindset is a continuous journey. Start with small steps and gradually incorporate these habits into your daily lifestyle to achieve your goals and reach your full potential.

Do not set limits on your unlimited potential. -W, Isdom

Chapter 14

Understanding Metrics

As a high school student, it's crucial to develop a comprehensive understanding of life metrics—important measures that can help you navigate your personal and academic life effectively. Life metrics encompass various aspects of your well-being, productivity, and personal growth. By understanding and tracking these metrics, you can make informed decisions, set meaningful goals, and strive for a balanced and fulfilling life.

I hope by now you are beginning to comprehend and enjoy the intricacies of owning a 'Middie Mindset.' Furthermore, let's dive into some essential life metrics and practical tips on how to measure and improve them.

Academic Metrics:

a. **Grade Point Average (GPA):**

- Understanding the grading scale and GPA calculation.
- Maintain a good GPA for college admissions.
- Focus on strategies for improving your GPA.

b. **Class Rank:**

- Understanding the significance and why it's important.
- Understand the pros of being ranked highly in your class.
  see Jalen Brown, University of California.
- Always aim high, not for recognition, but for positioning. *(Fire)*

c. Standardized Test Scores:

- Understanding the SAT, ACT, and other standardized tests.
- Know the scaling of test scores for college applications.
- Take classes and use study groups for preparing and improving test scores.

Time Management Metrics:

a. **Productivity:**

- Know the importance of effective time management. *(Highly Important)*
- Incorporate different techniques for prioritizing tasks and managing deadlines.
- Use smart technology to help scheduling. This will boost productivity.

b. **Procrastination:**

- Identifying signs of procrastination. *(Excuses)*
- Come up with different strategies to overcome procrastination and enhance productivity.
- Always work on mental fortitude and set realistic goals.

Lazy will get lapped. –G, Mack

Well-Being Metrics:

a. Sleep:

- Recovery, promoting better physical and mental performance for the next day.
- You should rest at least 7 hours each night.
- Create and maintain a healthy sleep routine. This includes napping. *(After school) lol.*

b. Physical Activity:

- Note that there are many benefits surrounding regular exercise physically and mentally.
    - Stress Prevention
    - Improve memory and brain function
    - Weight Management
    - Reduce anxiety and depression
- Incorporate physical activity into your daily routine so that it becomes a lifestyle.
- Find activities that you enjoy.

c. Nutrition:

- The impact of a balanced diet is imperative to your overall health.
- Make healthy food choices at school and home. Reduce sugar and high fructose intake.
- Avoid excessive junk food and sodas.

Personal Growth Metrics:

1. Extracurricular Activities:

- It is highly recommended to become involved in school clubs, sports, and community-based programs. This produces communications skills, and how to work in a team setting.
- Identify activities that align with your interests and goals.
- Be sure to create a balance between extracurricular and academics.

2. Leadership and Initiative:

- First rule of thumb, learn from failures and setbacks.
- Never shy away from opportunities to take the

leadership roles within your school or community.
- Innovation, efficiency, and quality. Effective, and persistent.

Five P's of Effective Leadership

1. Polite
2. Persistent
3. Patient
4. Present
5. Passionate

1. **Personal Reflection:**

- How do you see yourself is the beginning of self-reflection for personal growth.
- Journaling and mindfulness techniques.
- This is where discipline and intentionality comes into play. Analyze yourself at a Macro and Micro level to bring out the best version of you.

Without self-reflection, you will find yourself going through life without thinking, moving from one thing to the next without making time to evaluate things top to bottom. This means pause to think, to analyze, to determine what is going well and what isn't working. The unfortunate result is that most will shy away from taking out time to study oneself.

Reflection is a deeper form of learning that allows us to retain every aspect of any experience, be it personal or professional —why something took place, what the impact was, whether it should happen again —as opposed to just remembering that it happened. It's about tapping into every aspect of the experience, clarifying your thinking, and honing in on what really matters to you!

It is not by muscle, speed or physical dexterity that great things are achieved, but by reflection, force of character, and judgment. –Cicero

The Life Metrics

There will soon come a time when you will walk across the stage and toss your hat and tassels in the air. 12 years of grade school life, highs, and lows, forming relationships with classmates who will become lifelong friends. Making the transition into adulthood will come with new outlooks on life. Your life lenses will change. Before you knew what a Mindset was or a paradigm shift, it begins to happen on its on. Those who understand seasons understand change. Change is always good. It removes you from your comfort zone, allows the new to educate. So, with that being said let's take a look into *The Life Metrics.* Life metrics are Quantitative or Qualitative measures used to assess various aspects of an individual's life. These metrics can provide insights into the overall well-being, satisfaction, and success of a person in different areas of their life. Here are some commonly used life metrics:

1. **Happiness Index:** Measures the subjective well-being an contentment of an individual.

Define Yours:

____
____
____
____

2. **Quality of Life:** Evaluates the overall satisfaction and fulfillment in various domains of life, such as health, relationships, career, and leisure.

Define Yours:

____
____
____
____

3. **Health-Related Metrics:** Includes metrics like life expectancy, disease prevalence, physical fitness, and mental health indicators.

Define Yours:

____

____

____

____

4. **Financial Metrics:** Measures an individual's financial well-being, including income, savings, debt, and financial stability.

Define Yours:

____

____

____

____

5. Education and Knowledge: Considers metrics such as educational attainment, literacy rate, and access to educational resources.

Define Yours:

____

____

____

____

6. **Work-Life Balance:** Evaluates the ability to balance work commitments with personal life, leisure, and family time.

Define Yours:

____

____

____

____

7. **Social Connections:** Measures the strength and quality of an individual's relationships, social support network, and community involvement.

Define Yours:

____

____
____
____

9. **Personal Development:** Considers metrics related to self-improvement, learning, personal growth, and skills acquisition.

Define Yours:

____
____
____
____

10. **Civic Engagement:** Evaluates an individual's participation in community activities, volunteering, and political engagement. It's important to note that life metrics can vary depending on cultural, social, and individual contexts. Additionally, the interpretation and importance of these metrics can vary from person to person.

Define Yours:

____
____
____
____

Understanding and tracking Life Metrics can provide valuable insights into your academic performance, well being, and personal growth. By paying attention to these metrics, you can make informed choices, set realistic goals, and work towards a well-balanced and successful high school experience. Remember, everyone's journey is unique, and it is important to prioritize your top-to-bottom while striving for personal and academic growth.

Begin, be bold, and venture to be wise. – Horace

Chapter 15

BE

Be, determined to always do your best. Give 110% in all you do.

Be, teachable, be a student for life.

Be, careful to be perfect. Embrace your shortcomings, your flaws.

Be, respectful.

Be, kind, outgoing, be likeable.

Be, bold in your skin.

Be, wise and stay inquisitive.

Be, patient. Don't chase after life. She is much faster than you'll ever be.

Be, honest, transparent.

Be, creative.

Be, open to explore.

Be, the first to show up and the last to leave.

Be, the best version of yourself everyday.

Be, a difference maker.

Be, optimistic and fly high.

Be, spiritually connected with God.

Be, slow to anger.

Be, quiet in the cut, but very observant.

Be, a critical thinker.

Be, unapologetic when you believe in something.

Be, able to shift when the times call for it.

Be, full of love.

Be, true to your culture.

Be, outstanding even when you are sitting. –*G, Mack*

Be, brave.

Be, the solution to a problem.

Be, well versed.

Be, a lender and not a barrower.

Be, a good speaker.

Be, thoughtful.

Be, original.

Be, somewhere rather than everywhere. –*G, Mack*

Be, intentional.

Be, calculated. Strategic.

Be, balanced.

Be, a good person.

Be, you. –*Kee, J*

Be, who they say you cannot be.

Be, is a powerful mantra to understand as you are growing daily and encapsulating a world of possibilities and personal growth. It is an invitation to embrace one's authentic self, to explore passions, and to cultivate a sense of purpose. Be, encourages you to be bold, to step outside your comfort zones, and to face challenges with resilience. It is a constant reminder to be kind, compassionate, and empathetic towards others, fostering meaningful connections as well as promoting a sense of community. Be, is about finding balance, nurturing both physical and mental stability. It's an encouragement to be curious, to embrace learning, and to pursue knowledge. Ultimately, Be empowers you to discover unique talents, to chase your dreams, and to strive for excellence while staying true to your core values.

Always be greater than the voices of doubt and division. –W, Isdom

-Be,

Chapter 16

10x

The things that have brought you to this current moment will keep you here.

What does that mean?

If you show up and do the exact same thing day after day it's possible that you will get growth. It's likely you will become a little better than the day before, let's call it linear leaps. But, in order to get exponential growth, leopard leaps, it's going to take you tugging daily at self-recreation, showing up a little different each day, and implementing the discipline tactic of pushing aside the things you do not need to do then taking a deep dive into the things that will bring you the most return. (10x)

***Self-Recreation**- The Power to recreate one's own self from scratch.

Now that you have reached the final chapter your old ways of thinking should be challenged. This book is intended for you as a teenager to grow, evolve, renew your thinking, and launch your dreams today! Ask yourself this, why not own a Middie Mindset? Now in the same vein ask yourself a deeper question, how much will it cost me not to own a Middie Mindset? Let's do some math. You go to grade school for 12 years and if you pursue higher education:

Associates- 14 years
Bachelors- 15-16 years
Masters- 16-17 years
PHD- 18-20 years

Now you being good at math that's 12 long years of getting up early, riding the school bus, school lunch, teacher after teacher, after teacher. Homework, homework, homework. Test, test, test. 12 long years! "I cant' wait until I graduate," yes we all have said it. So now, here is the question at hand, what type of return should you get on your 12-year investment?

Write it down,

____
____
____
____
____
____
____

10x Thinking refers to a mindset of aiming for exponential growth or improvement rather than incremental progress. It encourages one to think bigger, push boundaries, and come up with innovative solutions. To every thing in life it's levels. In order to be a recipient of an abundant life filled with constant elevation you have to understand what type of return you want on your investment.

1. **Academic Goals:** Set academic goals that challenges you to achieve ten times more than your current performance. If your GPA is a [3.2] why not strive for a [4.0]? Better yet, [4.2]?

2. **Creating a Socially Conscious Business:** Start a business that not only generates profits but also addresses a specific social or environmental challenge. For instance, establishing a company that manufactures eco-friendly products, promotes financial liberty, or donates a portion of its profits to a charitable cause. Thinking this way early on equals to a lifelong return.

3. **Inventing a Breakthrough Technology:** Consider the emerging fields of technology, such as artificial intelligence, virtual reality, or gaming, and explore ways to leverage these technologies to create something revolutionary. This could

involve designing a new app, inventing a life-saving medical device, or simply finding the unmet needs.

4. **Disrupting an Existing Industry:** Identify an industry that could benefit from transformation and come up with a disruptive idea that challenges the status quo. For example, reimagining transportation by developing an affordable electric bike or designing an online platform that revolutionizes the way people buy and sell used goods. What are some examples of macroeconomics you know of?

____

____

____

____

____

____

____

5. **Influencing On Social Media Platforms:** *(Youtube)* Choose a meaningful topic that will highlight your strong suit. Research and educate yourself while creating compelling content. Be authentic and collaborate with like-minded influencers. Stay informed and use your platform responsibly while engaging with a global audience.

6. **Building Your Brand:** Always promote yourself, your style, your vision. Bring your creativity to life and share it with the world. Study those who have built successful brands. Be unique and find a mentor to help you understand the business side of building a brand. It's your idea, but it is also your job to make others love it!

7. **Innovating Arts and Culture:** Explore creative fields such as music, film, literature, or visual arts, and challenge traditional norms by experimenting with new styles, techniques, or mediums. Think about ways to use art to provoke thought, inspire change, or bring attention to social issues.

8. **Impactful Projects:** When working on projects or assignments, go beyond the minimum requirements and create something that leaves a significant impact. *(VERY IMPORTANT)*

9. **Career Aspirations:** Explore career paths and goals that not only provide financial stability but also allow you to make a meaningful difference in the world. Be a difference maker.

10. **Networking:** Build a network of mentors, peers, and professionals who can help you think bigger and provide guidance on your journey.

** Vision is the art of seeing what is invisible to others, –W, Isdom*

Remember, 10x thinking is about pushing boundaries, thinking creatively, and aiming for significant impact. It's about dreaming big, taking risks, and pursuing your passions while also considering the ethical and social implications of your ideas.

It is also the concept of aiming for goals that are ten times harder to achieve. It's the idea of continuously pushing your limits to achieve more than you initially believe to be possible. So again, what type of return should you want on your 12-year, grade school investment? *(1x, 6x, 9x,)?*

Still don't get it! Ok, let do it this way using the same number 12. Let's say you invest $12,000 into a new tech startup. How much would you agree to on your return? Time to test your math skills.

$10,000= ________________X Return?

$13,500= ________________X Return?

$20,000= ________________X Return?

$60,000= ________________X Return?

Example of 10x Return:

Initial investment: $12,000 Return multiplier:

10x to calculate the return, you would multiply the initial investment by the return multiplier:

Return = Initial investment * Return multiplier Return = $12,000 * 10

Return = $120,000

Therefore, a 10x return on a $12,000 tech startup investment would result in a total value of $120,000.

So I ask you one last time, what type of return would you like to receive on your 12-year investment?

Owning a Middie Mindset is the pathway to a 10x future. —G, Mack

10x Evolution

Evolution – any net directional change or cumulative change in characteristics of organisms or mindset modification.

The great Kobe Bryant once said that when he was 13-years-old he had a check-off-list. As an 8th grade basketball player he searched the Street & Smith basketball rankings list and his name was nowhere to be found within the top 50 player. Finally he saw his name at 57th. Playing his proxy he said to himself, *I can no longer show up everyday and do the same thing expecting different results. I have to focus on my weaknesses, self-recreation, become more inquisitive, watch more film in order to move up on the list. Once I do that I'm going to find each guy who is ranked higher than myself and introduce them to the new me. Not Kobe, Mr. Bryant!* And that is exactly what he did, but not only that by the time he was a senior he was the number one high school basketball player in the country. Knowing at an early age is key. Kobe was 13 years of age when he decided that a 1x, 5x, or even an 8x, was not good enough. He understood that in order to get the highest return on his investment he would have to study harder, listen harder, ask tougher questions, challenge his grit and face giants he was told he could not defeat. By doing so he was selected 13th in the first round of the 1996 NBA draft. His first year in the NBA he was nothing to brag about. Again, he tapped back in to his understanding of what it would take to become not just a good NBA player, but a great NBA player. Kobe Bryant went on to win 5 NBA championships and became the only player in the modern day era to score 81 points in a single game second to Wilt Chamberland's 100 points.

Was it the fact that he grew to 6'7? Was it the fact that his dad was a retired NBA player? Or was it that he was just one of the lucky ones? No, No, No! It was his MINDSET! He adopted the slogan: *Mamba Mentality*. This is equivalent to what you are adopting today, a Middie Mindset. *Middie Mentality*. All that you have read and studied isn't just words on paper, it's a mentality that must be taken seriously. A very high percentage of the people the world follows on Social Media, NBA, WNBA, MLS, Entertainers and Political Figures, all own a Middie Mindset. It's not by happenstance that they are where they are. It took discipline. Locking in and breaking the key off in the lock. *(Forever Locked In)*. They understood the assignment and knew that in order to penetrate any business and or industry they had to follow a specific set of rules that was set before they became.

- Understand the nature of a thing.
- Understand that in order to become, I must begin.
- Become a great listener.
- Study, fail, study, execute.
- Only do the things that will help me grow in this area.
- Own a Mindset that is not easily shifted, nor uprooted.

It behooves you as a teenager to learn to love to listen. Learn to love to push pass your limits. Learn to love to be the best version of yourself ever single second of the day. Why not? Why wait until you are 25, 35, 40 years-old to say, "ok, I'm ready now." Study says that it takes the human brain 25 years to fully develop. Knowing this, I would love for you to start setting goals now!

By the age 25 I am going to:

Push- Push- Push, beyond your comfort zones and I guarantee that you will experience a significant growth and reap a harvest of many accomplishment. The Middie Mindset coupled with resilience = 10x evolution.

Today I want you to vow to always embrace challenges, learn from mistakes and failures, and promise yourself that you will always bounce back from setbacks. You will listen, you will be honest, you will be respectful, you will love hard, and you will always keep God first.

Tomorrow is your baby, nurture her, respect her, and promise her that you will accept nothing short of a 10x return on your investment.

Congratulations,
Recipient of a Middie Mindset

Name_____________________________

Date______________________________

About The Author

Gerald Mack is an acclaimed author from Middletown, Ohio. An owner of many gifts and talents, his focus is helping to build up his community and assisting the youth in discovering their true identity. Passion and purpose is the law he lives by. God first, followed by love, a solid foundation he stands upon.

Why The Title Middie Mindset?

A small town engulfed between Cincinnati and Dayton, Ohio better known as Middletown. Under 70,000 in population, yet our little town is known across the globe. How so?

For beginners, at one point of time in the 1980's Douglass Park was ranked as one of the top street ball courts to play at in the U.S.

Then there is a place called Middletown High School, home to the Middies! *(Purple and White)* A school that has produced the likes of NBA Top 50 Great: **Jerry Lucas.** NBA Rookie of The Year. *(63-64)* NBA Championship: *(New York Knicks 1973)*

Cris Carter, one of the greatest wide receivers to ever play in the NFL. *(Hall of Fame)* Younger brother to another Middie great, **Butch Carter.** *(NBA Player. NBA Coach)*

Todd Bell, Ohio State / Chicago Bears *(81-84)*

Jalin Marshall, Ohio State, 2015 College Football National Championship. / New York Jets

Jeff Cothran, Ohio State / Cincinnati Bengals.

Bill Edwards, Philadelphia 76ers, overseas basketball legend. Wright State University all time leading scorer.

Kayla Harrison, (MMA) Olympic Gold *(2012 & 2016)* Pan American Gold *(2011 & 2015)*

Kyle Schwaber, (MLB) World Series 2016. **Chicago Cubs*

J.D. Vance, Author of the Memoir, 'Hillbilly Elegy' *(Netflix)* Republican Senator, Ohio.

Victor McFarlane, Founder and Executive Chairman of McFarlane Partners.

Stephen Hightower, Founder and CEO of Hightowers Petroleum.

Dr. Rahsaan Lindsey, Psychiatrist: Arizona Cardinals / Arizona Diamondbacks.

Siraaj Hasan, Principal Director – Booz Allen Hamilton.
Founder: *Lifting As We Climb foundation.* Co-Founder: *Sound Mind-Sound Body foundation.*

These are just a few of the Middletown Middie Legends. There are many more that graced the hallways, grade A in the classrooms, and dominated in sports creating a legacy and paving the way for the generations after them. The one thing that the few names I mentioned have in common is their Mindset. It takes a certain level of discipline, moxie and sweat equity to make it to the top of your game. To become a champion! You know how hard it is to make it to an elite level? Olympic Champion... NBA Champion... NFL Hall of Fame... Executive Chairman... Psychiatrist for two Pro teams? Do you understand what type of Mindset you have to own? We live in a United States full of talented, smart, strong, hungry, and dedicated people. Not to include those over seas. Yet all fighting for a position. Training for years for the opportunity to showcase their skillsets.

Nevertheless, it is more to it than that. Now it becomes a numbers game. Let's use the NBA for an example, 30 teams, 15 players, 13 which can be active for each game. 30 x 15= 450. Wait; so you mean to tell me out of all the young men who grow up with aspirations to play in the NBA, there are only 450 spots available? My bad, the majority of those spots are already taken. Now we have to crunch those numbers. Each year the NBA has a draft. This draft consists of picking some of the top college and overseas players. It get's deeper, there are only 2 rounds. 1st Round = 30 picks. 2nd Round = 30 picks. So those 450 spots are reduced to 60 spots. So now we have to understand that the 2nd Round picks aren't guaranteed. There is a strong chance that you may not make the roster. So at the end of the day you have millions of young men playing basketball in the U.S. and a few more million in other countries, let's say 100M+ training, breathing, sleeping, fighting for 60 spots. Approximately 1.67 million to 1, which means securing a spot is very slim! **Elite level can never own a Mediocre Mindset.** Especially if we are talking about chasing a dream that only has 60 available positions.

As a top tier high school running back Jeff Cothran understood the assignment. The journey is uphill and the NFL positions are few. After rigorous days of football practice Jeff would opt out from catching rides home. Instead he would run five miles to complete the day.

Cris Carter was asked why was he up running hills so early? His response was, "because the west coast is three hours behind and Jerry Rice isn't woke yet." That's a prime example of a Middie Mindset.

In every city and small town our youth wake up each day with aspirations to become better. We live in a society where some of the music, certain channels, social media and peer-to-peer interactions send out the wrong messages. More of the reason for a new way of thinking and information to come to the light. The goal is to intercept the young minds that find themselves ensnared in low vibrating settings. Once the mind adopts the right principles and learn how to think on an elite level it's game over. I'd be remised if I did not offer a book with the keys to unlocking the potential for high school success. Lifelong success. So here we have it, that's why I call it *'Middie Mindset.'* It's not about one school, one team, one culture, it's about motivating all schools, all teams, all cultures, and all students to push pass limits and find out how great you can become. **Be inspired, stay dope, be blessed.** *-G, Mack.*

Made in United States
Orlando, FL
12 May 2024